Writing is a gift that God placed in your heart . . . a special part of who you are. Let it inspire you . . . and never give up.

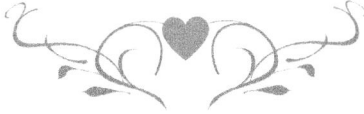

This Everyday Journal was made for you by an author who received her first journal at a young age and has been writing ever since.

Lyn D. Nielsen embraces drama, adventure, and mystery to inspire her readers through life.

Discover her books at: www.lyndnielsen.com, and join the Place of Sage Family!

Published in the United States by Place of Sage Books
Soap Lake, Washington

ISBN: 978-1-7372516-7-5

Made in the USA
Las Vegas, NV
19 March 2022